NIMAL SUPERPOWERS
SHAPESHIFTING
BY MONIKA DAVIES
T0394785
EPIC
BELLWETHER MEDIA ★ MINNEAPOLIS, MN

EPIC BOOKS are no ordinary books. They burst with intense action, high-speed heroics, and shadows of the unknown. Are you ready for an Epic adventure?

This edition first published in 2026 by Bellwether Media, Inc.

Library of Congress Cataloging-in-Publication Data

LC record for Shapeshifting available at: https://lccn.loc.gov/2025021801

Editor: Rachael Barnes Designer: Gabriel Hilger

Printed in the United States of America, North Mankato, MN.

TABLE OF CONTENTS

CHANGING APPEARANCES

Some animals can change their size and shape. These animals can **transform** how they look in seconds!

Some shift their shape to hide. Others change to scare off **predators**.

THE TRANSFORMER

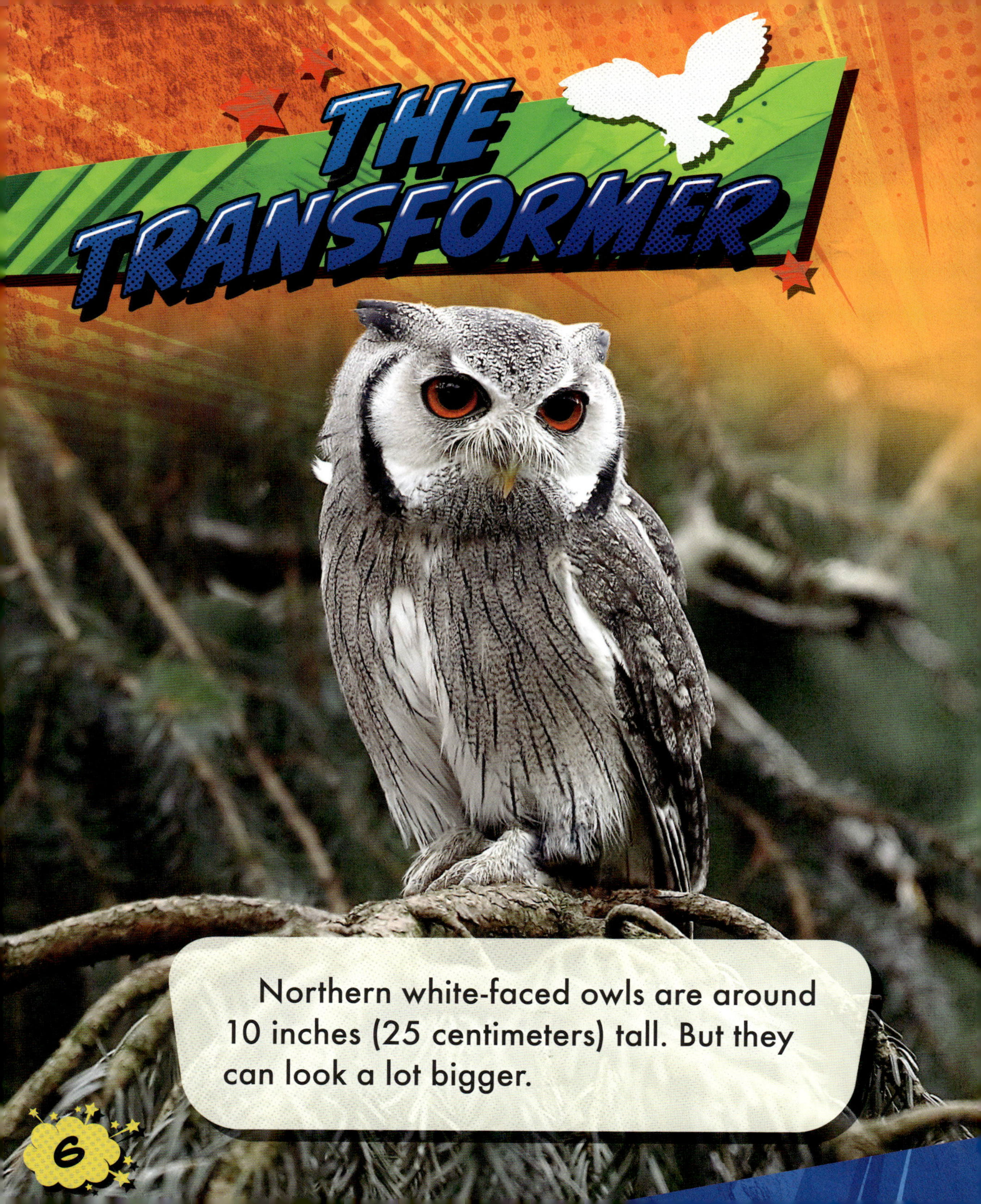

Northern white-faced owls are around 10 inches (25 centimeters) tall. But they can look a lot bigger.

These owls open their wings wide. Feathers puff up all over their bodies. They scare small predators away!

NORTHERN WHITE-FACED OWL

CLASS: BIRD

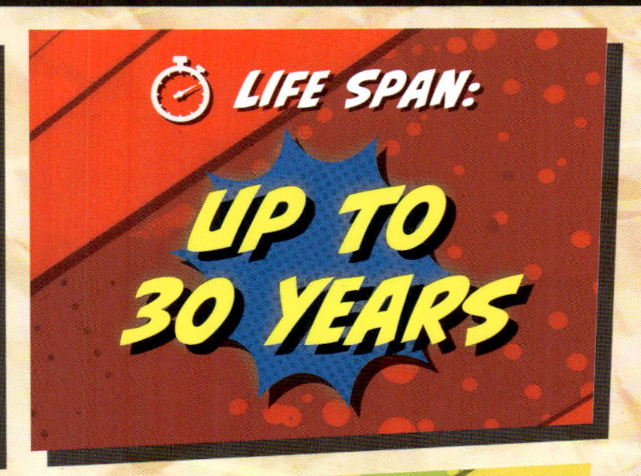

STATUS IN THE WILD

RANGE

Large predators such as hornbills also hunt these owls. Northern white-faced owls **shrink** to hide from their attacks.

These transforming owls pull in their feathers. They stand up tall to look thinner. They blend into the trees!

THE WATER BALLOON

Puffer fish have stiff bodies. They are slow swimmers. They use their fins and tail to move.

Puffer fish have a special skill to stay safe. They can quickly grow in size!

GUINEAFOWL PUFFER FISH

STATUS IN THE WILD

LEAST CONCERN	NEAR THREATENED	VULNERABLE	ENDANGERED	CRITICALLY ENDANGERED	EXTINCT IN THE WILD	EXTINCT

When enemies are nearby, puffer fish can suck in water. Their stomachs **expand**. They blow up to four times their size in seconds!

Round puffer fish are hard to swallow. Predators stay away.
A HARMFUL SNACK
Most puffer fish have poison in different body parts! Eating them will hurt most predators.

THE PUNK ROCKER

Mutable rainfrogs are about the size of a fingernail. These frogs are found in **cloud forests** in Ecuador.

They often sit on moss. Their skin **texture** is spiky to match. They are nicknamed punk rockers!

MUTABLE RAINFROG

CLASS: AMPHIBIAN

LIFE SPAN:

UNKNOWN

STATUS IN THE WILD

LEAST CONCERN	NEAR THREATENED	VULNERABLE	ENDANGERED	CRITICALLY ENDANGERED	EXTINCT IN THE WILD	EXTINCT

RANGE

Their spiky skin stands out on smooth surfaces. Mutable rainfrogs change their skin to blend in!

Their skin can become smooth in minutes. They stay hidden.
A RECENT FIND
Scientists first spotted a mutable rainfrog in 2006. It took three years to find one again!

THE COPYCAT

Mimic octopuses are tricksters! They change to look like other ocean animals.

Mimic octopuses can change the color and pattern of their skin. That octopus looks like a sea snake!

MIMIC OCTOPUS

CLASS: INVERTEBRATE

LIFE SPAN:

UP TO 2 YEARS

STATUS IN THE WILD

LEAST CONCERN	NEAR THREATENED	VULNERABLE	ENDANGERED	CRITICALLY ENDANGERED	EXTINCT IN THE WILD	EXTINCT

RANGE

N
W
E
S

Mimic octopuses change their shape, too. They fold, hide, or spread out their arms. They try to match the look of **poisonous** animals.

Shapeshifters are hard to spot.
They are masters of **disguise**!

cloud forests—mountain forests that are wet and cloudy

disguise—an outward appearance that hides what something really is

expand—to increase in size

mimic—related to closely copying

poisonous—causes illness or death when it enters or touches the body

predators—animals that hunt other animals for food

shrink—to make smaller

texture—the way something looks or feels

transform—to change

TO LEARN MORE

AT THE LIBRARY

Davies, Monika. *Invisibility.* Minnetonka, Minn.: Bellwether Media, 2026.

Loh-Hagan, Virginia. *Wild Disguises.* Ann Arbor, Mich.: 45th Parallel Press, 2023.

Riggs, Kate. *Octopuses.* Mankato, Minn.: Creative Education and Creative Paperbacks, 2025.

ON THE WEB

FACTSURFER

Factsurfer.com gives you a safe, fun way to find more information.

1. Go to www.factsurfer.com.
2. Enter "shapeshifting" into the search box and click 🔍.
3. Select your book cover to see a list of related content.

INDEX

The images in this book are reproduced through the courtesy of: Guy Edwardes Photography/ Alamy Stock Photo, front cover, p. 7 (class: bird); sci, p. 3; David Fleetham/ Alamy Stock Photo, pp. 4, 11 (inset), 13, 21 (banded sea snake); 義生 大沢, p. 5; Ger Bosma/ Alamy Stock Photo, p. 6; Zoo-Life/ Alamy Stock Photo, p. 7 (inset); Emily, p. 8 (hornbill); Oliver Smart/ Alamy Stock Photo, p. 8; FLPA/ Alamy Stock Photo, p. 9; f9photos, p. 10; Elena, p. 11 (class: fish); Luigi, p. 12; Jeff Rotman/ Alamy Stock Photo, p. 12 (expanded); Anton Sorokin/ Alamy Stock Photo, p. 14; Morley Read/ Alamy Stock Photo, pp. 15 (inset, class: amphibian), 16; Morley Read/ Minden, p. 17; Alex Mustard/ Minden, p. 18; Brandon Cole Marine Photography/ Alamy Stock Photo, pp. 19 (inset), 21 (lionfish); Francesco, p. 19 (class: invertebrate); Avalon.red/ Alamy Stock Photo, p. 20-21; Joe Belanger, p. 21 (mimic octopus); Ethan Daniels, p. 21 (banded sole); Nature Picture Library/ Alamy Stock Photo, p. 23.